TERRITORIAL SPIRITS

Overcome Evil Strongholds in Your Life And Take Over Your Community With Strategic Warfare And Winning Prayers

JOHANNES TEFO

Territorial Spirits: Overcome Evil Strongholds in Your Life And Take Over Your Community With Strategic Warfare And Winning Prayers

Johannes Tefo

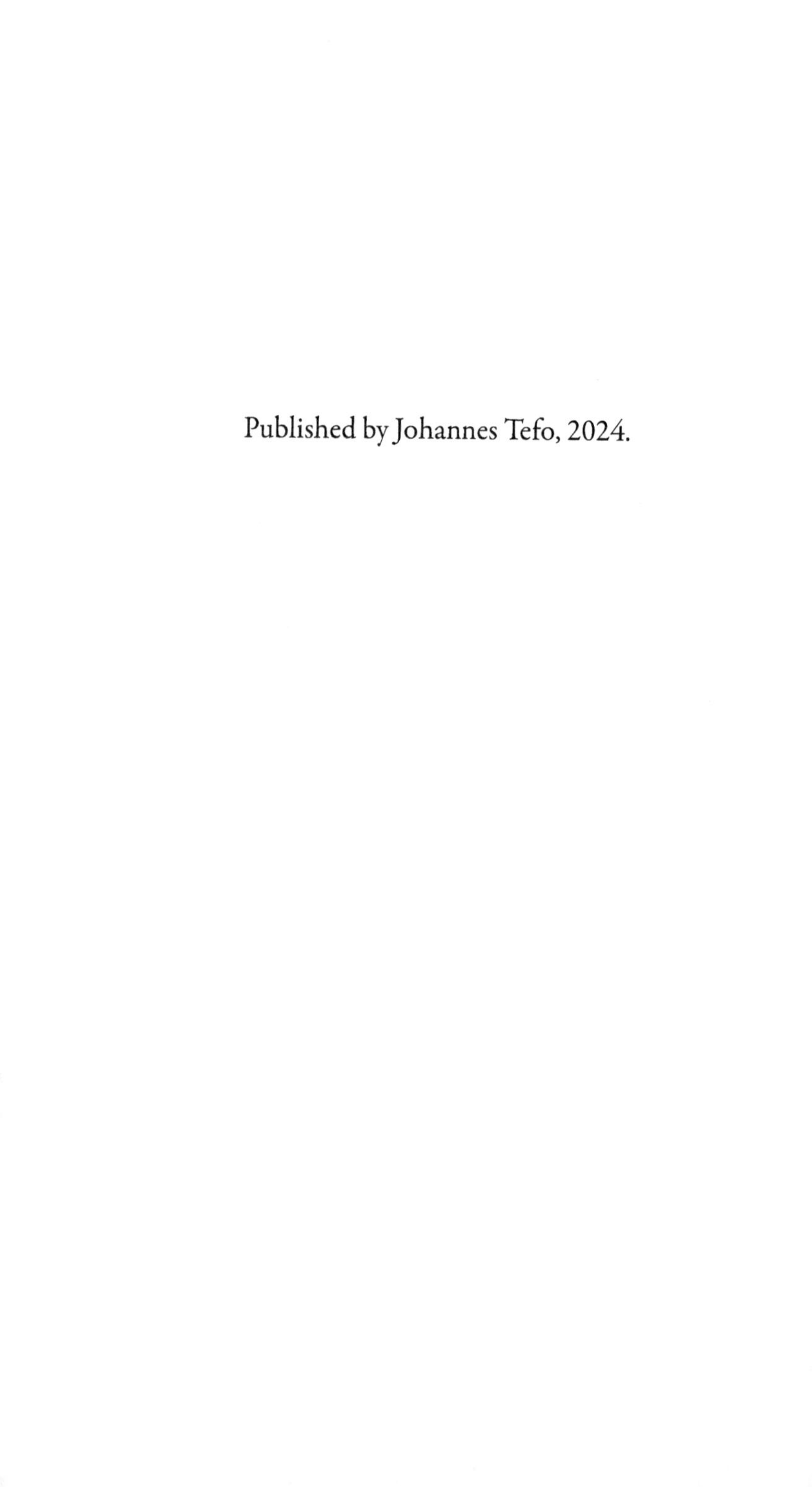

Published by Johannes Tefo, 2024.

Also by Johannes Tefo

Family spiritual Warfare Books
Youth's Guide To Spiritual Warfare
A Women's Guide To Spiritual Warfare

Standalone
Deliver Your Soul From Evil: Self Deliverance Guide
Deliverance From Mind Control: Be Free And Delivered
From Every Marine Demons Of Mind Control
Overcoming Spirit Of Stagnation
The 24: Prophetic Word For This Season 2024 And Beyond
Michael For Warfare
Territorial Spirits: Overcome Evil Strongholds in Your Life
And Take Over Your Community With Strategic Warfare
And Winning Prayers

Table of Contents

I dedicated this book to the body of Christ!

To God be the glory, power, and honor, amen!

Introduction

This is what many dare to teach. It may be because of a lack of knowledge and understanding of this subject of territorial spirits. Growing up I used to have a lot of vivid dreams and visions, unbeknown that they were ushering me into a prophetic ministry. Especially in the sky, I would see princes, princesses, angels, or normal people like us descending from heaven. Some I will have conversations with, some I will not, it would be like objective vision, whereby you are just witnessing the event.

I would see thick clouds moving, and at some point, I would see different animal-like creatures within. Animals in the spirit represent witchcraft, especially domestic animals while wild animals represent the highest level of occult and witchcraft. By the way, I also come from a village that is big in witchcraft practices. My whole family lineage was affected by witches and wizards. While some died being victims of it.

You cannot deny the effect or the power of Satan. We as the body of Christ sometimes undermine the power of the enemy. We are victorious in Christ. But to tell you the truth, Jesus Christ never undermined Satan. In fact, He called him the prince of this world. And other names like "The God of this world and "The prince of the power of the air".

Yes, in the realm of the spirit world, Satan is a prince. I believe he is in a different league because he is called "The Anointed Cherub" in the bible. Other angels are not called 'anointed'. As much as we cannot deny the evil powers of the Devil, we also cannot deny witchcraft powers. This is what some of my family members did, they were ignorant of the demonic spirit world even though you can tell that something fishy is up.

Whether you can act civil or not, Satan and his hosts of evil are at work in this day and age. The Devil has been working since his fall from grace. He is a furious and wrath man because he is in a lower state than he was in heaven. He is the enemy of the will of God. And he is against you child of God—to turn you from the righteous path of the Almighty God.

The sorrows he brought to Job's life, he is unleashing it into our lives. We must never be fooled since windy doctrines teach that Lucifer is the light-bearer of hidden wisdom and knowledge. Entities like Illuminate and Freemasonry uphold him in great honor and will likely tell you that there are different personalities between Lucifer and Satan. I tell you, they are the same, he was Lucifer in heaven, and Satan is the character he took. Satan means deceiver or adversary.

In this profound spiritual warfare book, these are the main things I talk about below. I believe these are what you need to foster victory in your life and in the lives of people around you. Territorial powers are real. And many are the victims of stagnation and a cycle of perpetual misfortunes because of evil powers in the sky. Satan is the god of this world. And the Bible also goes on to say that He is the prince of the power of the air. He has more influence on this world than many think. Though he is limited because he is not omnipresent like King Jesus.

1. **Prayer:** Prayer is a powerful tool that you can use to connect with God and ask for His protection and guidance. Through prayer, you can ask for strength to

resist temptation and courage to stand up against the wiles of the devil.

2. **The Word of God:** Reading and studying the Bible can help you gain a deeper understanding of God's teachings and develop a stronger spiritual foundation. The Bible will provide you with guidance on how to resist temptation and overcome spiritual challenges.

3. **Fasting:** Fasting involves abstaining from food or other pleasures for a period of time as a way to focus on spiritual growth. You may use fasting as a way to strengthen your faith and resist temptation.

4. **Fellowship:** Connecting with other believers through worship, prayer, and other activities can provide you with support and encouragement, especially during satanic attacks. Fellowship can also help Christians stay accountable to their spiritual goals and provide a sense of community.

5. **Forgiveness:** Forgiving others and seeking forgiveness for one's own mistakes can be a powerful way to overcome negative influences and strengthen one's spiritual connection with God.

6. **Worship:** Worshiping God through music, prayer, and other activities can help you focus on your spiritual connection with God and resist negative influences from the god of this age since mind control is what is aiming for.

7. **Love:** Showing love and compassion to others, even in the face of adversity, can be a powerful way to resist negative influences and strengthen one's faith.

The unseen realm is more real than you think. I am glad these days Christians and non-believers all over the world are awakening to the unseen realm. Revelatory knowledge is unveiled before our own eyes like never before. We are living in the age prophesized by Daniel that in the last days knowledge shall increase.

With all that said, I am not implying that the devil is anywhere near or equal to God. But you can feel, sense, and see his presence, which will at times be the opposite of what God does.

With so many spiritual revelations, technology, and science at rocket heights, the enemy is also at the door to offer something that feels godly while it is not. From inception, the enemy has long been rival with the human race trying to substitute the government of God in our lives with his own kingdom that looks appealing but deadlier than a cobra's venom.

The aim of this personality called, Satan, is to kill, steal, and destroy. To divert the call of God and dilute the fire within our hearts with evil sensations. But glory to God since many around the world are waking up from their sleep of death which is spiritual ignorance. Ignorance of the things of the holy spirit in our lives will cost us a lot. The saving grace of the Living God is limited when there is a high level of ignorance of the voice of God.

Isaiah 55 says harken unto my words you shall live and eat. Prosperity and success come from being sensible to the voice of God and doing what He tells you to do. You can name them; healing, deliverance, miracles, and so on, they all manifest through the power of the word of God. Harkening to the voice of the Living God increases our faith for us to be bold like lions and release words that translate to tangible things in the physical world. This beautiful world of ours is built upon faith. It was by faith that Elohim spoke this world into existence. Remember that you are walking on a spiritual earth, found by spiritual principles of God—called faith.

When we are engaging in spiritual warfare, the weapons we use are spiritual weapons. Apostle Paul wrote for us a perfect and holy spirit-inspired hierarchy of the dominion of the kingdom of darkness—powers and thrones in high places, rulers of spiritual darkness of this world, and principalities in heavenly places. I grew up with phony teaching that says the devil lives in hell.

From the spiritual encounters I have had throughout my walk with God, I can without a doubt tell that the devil has dominion or kingdom in hell but does not live in hell. He has three dominions; the high places in the heavenly, the marine kingdom under the sea, and hades or hell in the underworld. These three kingdoms' mission is to deceive, manipulate, and control the inhabitants of the earth, people, animals, and world system.

His main mission is to turn this world into satanic worship assisted by other fallen angels, demons, and human agents who sold their souls to the dark science of the kingdom of darkness. Though, he is not all-powerful since he is not omniscient like God. He can only be at one spot at a time. This is one of his weaknesses. The kingdom is strengthened by its unity, its hierarchy structure, and many people around the nations following this worldly system in their mentality, deeds, and actions opposing the Holy Spirit.

The truth of God is what shall set the people of this world free. Christ is that covenant to the nations of the earth to purge us with his precious holy blood.

2 Chronicles 7:14 If my people, which are called by my name, shall humble themselves, and pray, and seek my face, and turn from their wicked ways; then will I hear from heaven, and will forgive their sin, and will heal their land.

This is the secret to warfare. When this scripture says *"Shall humble themselves"* here it talks about prayer and fasting. By the way, fasting is an act of humility before the presence of God.

Prayer will always be on top of the list as a weapon of warfare and deliverance. There is basically nothing you can do without a life of prayer. Not only prayer but strategic and serious prayers that put you on the spot in every kingdom. The kingdom of God backs up warriors in Christ. Same applies, the kingdom of the enemy seeks after the souls of prayer warriors to steal, kill, and destroy.

This battle did not start in the Garden of Eden. It started in heaven where archangel Michael was ordered to cast down Lucifer from heaven. Actually, he was Lucifer before he became Satan—the deceiver. The world Satan describes his motive and action.

Isaiah 14 and Ezekiel 28 give a detailed description of his fall. The root of his fall was pride and rebellion—and iniquity was found in him. He was no longer fit to be before the presence of God through his dealings. Dealings can refer to connection, transitions, or business. Any man who has had an encounter with this dark prince had to bargain with him. Look how our mainstream celebrities are not even ashamed to flash out their ties with this personality. Even worse, our so-called men of God and women of God are also following the same route.

I had deep revelations about men and women of God who sold their souls to the dark side for fame, power, and money. Some will go around looking for power to demonstrate miracles, healing, and deliverance in churches. For the most part, it is all deception. As someone who was unknowingly initiated into occultism in church, I can without a doubt attest that many pastors, prophets, apostles, and bishops serve the god of mammoth(money). They use church members to raise funds for their lavish lifestyles.

Every individual must study the bible to show themselves approved. This is a set time for the move of God and the enemy knows it. The enemy is unleashing dark forces like never before to limit us from reaching the spiritual height God set out for us. The spirit of religion is blinding many with dark blinders to never see the truth. We must allow the holy spirit to eliminate all the religious cultural traditions of man-made doctrines. The battle is on.

The battlefield of spiritual warfare is a place where the forces of light and darkness clash in a great and eternal struggle. For we wrestle not against flesh and blood, but against principalities, against powers, against the rulers of the darkness of this world, against spiritual wickedness in high places.

In this great battle, we must put on the whole armor of God, so that we may be able to stand against the wiles of the devil. We must gird our loins with truth, and put on the breastplate of righteousness. We must take the shield of faith, wherewith we shall be able to quench all the fiery darts of the wicked. And we must take the helmet of salvation, and the sword of the Spirit, which is the word of God.

For we know that the weapons of our warfare are not carnal, but mighty through God to the pulling down of strongholds. We know that we have not been given a spirit of fear, but of power, and of love, and of a sound mind. And we know that if God be for us, who can be against us?

Therefore, let us be strong in the Lord, and in the power of his might. Let us fight the good fight of faith, and lay hold on eternal life. Let us be steadfast, unmovable, always abounding in the work of the Lord. And let us not be weary in well doing, for in due season we shall reap if we faint not.

For the Lord is our refuge and our strength, a very present help in times of trouble. He is our shield and our buckler, our high tower and our fortress. He is the God of our salvation, in whom we trust. And he has promised that he will never leave us nor forsake us.

Therefore, let us go forth into the battlefield of spiritual warfare, knowing that we are not alone, but that the Lord is with us. Let us fight with all our might, and let us never give up the fight, for the victory is already won, and the crown of glory awaits those who are faithful unto the end.

Preparing war

As a follower of Christ, you are engaged in a spiritual battle that requires constant vigilance and preparation. The enemy is real, and he seeks to steal, kill, and destroy (John 10:10). However, do not be discouraged or afraid, for you have been given the power and authority to overcome the enemy (Luke 10:19).

To prepare for spiritual warfare, there are several things that you can do. Firstly, you need to know who you are in Christ. You are a child of God, redeemed by the blood of Jesus, and empowered by the Holy Spirit. You are loved, valued, and chosen by God (John 1:12, 1 Peter 2:9). Therefore, you must resist the lies of the enemy and hold onto the truth of God's Word.

Secondly, you need to put on the armor of God (Ephesians 6:10-18). The armor consists of the belt of truth, the breastplate of righteousness, the shoes of peace, the shield of faith, the helmet of salvation, and the sword of the Spirit, which is the Word of God. Each piece of armor represents a spiritual truth that you must apply in your life. For example, the belt of truth represents the need to know and live by the truth of God's Word.

Thirdly, you need to be in constant prayer and fellowship with God. Prayer is a powerful weapon in spiritual warfare (Ephesians 6:18). Through prayer, you can ask for protection, guidance, and strength. You can also intercede for others and pray against the schemes of the enemy. Additionally, regular fellowship with God through Bible reading, worship, and fellowship with other believers, strengthens your faith and helps you discern the voice of God.

Fourthly, you need to live a life of obedience and holiness. The enemy often uses sin and disobedience to gain a foothold in our lives. Therefore, it is important to repent of sin and strive for holiness. This means living a life that is pleasing to God and aligns with His Word. It also means avoiding things that are contrary to God's will and purpose for your life.

Finally, you need to stay alert and be prepared for spiritual attacks. The enemy does not give up easily and will often come at us when we least expect it. Therefore, it is important to be vigilant and watchful. When you sense an attack, pray for protection, and use the armor of God to defend yourself.

In conclusion, preparing for spiritual warfare requires a daily commitment to knowing God, putting on the armor of God, praying, living a life of obedience and holiness, and staying alert. Remember that you are not alone in this battle, for the Lord is with you (Isaiah 41:10). Stand firm in your faith, and trust in the Lord's power and protection.

May God bless you and keep you strong in the battle.

In Genesis 1:2 we are told that the earth was **"without form and void"** (in Hebrew, *tohu va bohu)*. This would indicate that the first of God's judgments took place between Genesis 1:1 and Genesis 1:2. Possibly it could have been a judgment on the original rebellion of Lucifer (Satan).

The battle did begin in heaven. It did not begin with a human being but with an archangel who has come to be known as Satan, although his original name was Lucifer. He had already alienated a numerous of the angels under his leadership before he turned his attention to the human race.

Genesis 3:1-13 records how Lucifer, appearing in the form of a serpent, approached Adam and Eve, the parents of the human race, and enticed them into rebellion. In response, God pronounced a prophetic judgment on Lucifer and on the woman:

So the Lord God said to the serpent: "Because you have done this, you are cursed more than all cattle, and more than every beast of the field; on your belly you shall go, and you shall eat dust all the days of your life. And I will put enmity between you and the woman, and between your seed and her Seed; He shall bruise your head, and you shall bruise His heel."

verses 14-15

I am with the firm believe that there were many civilizations before Adam. I am not saying Adam was not the first man, he was the first man to be created in the image and after the likeness of God. In the scriptures, we only see man created in the image of God. Psalm 8 says we were made a little lower than angels.

It fascinates me as an angel's main duty is to watch over the souls of men. There are many ranks in the angelic realm, we have worshipping angels who are around the throne, messengers like Gabriel, warfare leaders like archangel Michael, and more. All these angels look out for the activities of men. Man is the apple of God's eyes. The planet Earth is the center of God's attention. I have a firm believe that we have more grace than angels because when we sin, God forgives.

I bring you the result of study, meditation, prayer, and practical experience. In Genesis 6, we have an account of the sons of God who left their heavenly habitation—made an oath to sleep with women. God never forgave what they did. How amazing is His grace to us who are a little lower than them? To God be the glory. However, we are at a detriment because of these angels who are now called "fallen ones" since they are on the agenda of building walls between humans and their Maker.

It pained so much that we are sinful in nature as humans but God's mercy, grace, and goodness abound more in our lives. As a prophetic individual myself, at some point in time while worshipping and praising at night, my eyes opened, and I saw Azazel, the fallen angel in the second heaven. I heard him saying I reminded him while he was in the third heaven while he was worshipping and praising God.

A man is crowned with more glory and honor than any being ever created. You should at any point not think low of yourself. It is a pity when you see people taking their lives out—committing suicide over little challenges of life.

Genesis 1:1-2 In the beginning God created the heaven and the earth.

2 And the earth was without form, and void;
and darkness was upon the face
of the deep. And the Spirit of God moved upon the face of the waters.

Back in to pre-Adamic race, the earth was formless and void. There is a huge debate about the timeline of man on Earth and about how long has the earth been. These are the questions archeologists and scientists have been battling with for years due to their research findings that are deemed to be older than 6,000 years.

I strongly believe that the was civilizations before Adam, which are made up of strange beings caused by Lucifer's fall, are the reason why we see strange beings manifesting themselves all over the world. There was a world before man was created. We believe Adam is the first man and the first human being to ever grace the human race. While we may not know the timeline of the fall of Lucifer and angelic beings who mated with women, it goes to say that Lucifer was given a certain territory to rule. Basically, a dominion position.

Satan is not to be taken lightly as some pastors do in their preaching. Jesus Christ never underestimated Satan's power and influence over humankind. It would take the holy spirit of God that is in you to take Satan and demons down. I was startled at one time when the spirit of God revealed to me that demons are more intelligent than humans. Many do not know this. You will hear them taunting during deliverance sessions—Christ never interviewed demons in his ministry but cast them out.

We learn in Genesis that God told Adam to replenish the earth. *Re* means to do it again. God would have said plenish the earth if it was for the first time. While the Bible says Adam was the first man on earth, I also believe that there was another race here before Adam. Which I believe was a hybrid of different species and animals. The holy spirit spoke to me at one point that anything that is called mythology or folktale, was once in a lifetime. The gods were once on this earth. In South Africa where I am from, there is a huge stone with a footprint of a person and the footprint is huge. There is no human being on this earth with that kind of foot—close to one meter.

There is an undeniable evidence that a different race was once upon earth. I have also come across a mountain shaped like a human face. As someone who is prophetic, through the grace of God I have also traveled in spirit to see universes and other civilizations. I have seen the people from the sky and the marine life where there are people living.

When one thinks of the underground world, we think of hell, brimstones, fire, and pitch blackness. The righteous men and women who died before Jesus Christ came in this world, were dwelling in the place called Abraham's bosom. There is a side for the holy saints and for ungodly believers living in shame. Mind you, Abraham's bosom was not in heaven. The heavenly place where the redeemed are because of Christ is the paradise, located in the north direction. It is a third heaven where Apostle Paul was caught up in spirit.

If you can locate the direction of the north upwards, beyond it is the government of God led by Holy Jesus. Jesus Christ is the king. There will come a time in the near future when the dead in Christ will rise up. It has not happened yet.

Through dreams, visions, and out-of-body experiences, I have seen people in an old place called Abraham' bosom. Folks, it is not hell, there is hell on the other side. And people cannot see each other there. I was surprised because as believers of Christ, we know that when you go to that underworld, you have gone to hell period.

It is also written in Psalms that when Christ ascended, he also descended and led the captives free. These I believe, are the righteous saints who were worthy to be presented before the throne of God. The death of Jesus Christ not only delivered people on planet Earth but brought redemption to other worlds that we do not know.

The main aim of writing this chapter is to lay an argument that what happened during the fall of Lucifer and the sons of God who went to sleep with women, produced a different race of wickedness. The book of Enoch which is not part of the canon of the bible, has so much to say about these giants—Nephilim.

They corrupted the world. They introduced violence on earth. The children of men were at the mercy of these giants because they would eat up everything on farms leaving them with nothing to the point where they could no longer have food to sustain them and started eating human flesh. There was an abomination upon the planet Earth. Many still ask themselves why God ended the then lives with a flood.

It is because there was a lot of corruption. The blood of men and women was corrupted and mixed up to create different evil species. I believe that demons are the spirits of the children of these giants. It is a different hybrid of the blood of humans mixed with angelic DNA if there is such a thing.

S atan is referred to several times as the god of this age or the prince of the power of the air (Eph. 2:2; 2 Cor. 4:4).

The power [or authority] **of the air** refers to Satan's host of demons who exist in the heavenly sphere. Note, that spirits are flexible and are not constrained within time and space. They move swiftly within space and time. At one point the spirit of the Lord told me that spirits are more intelligent that humans because they are not restricted by time. They live in a timeless atmosphere. And they also study, and have been studying human beings for ages.

Paul has this in mind in Ephesians 6:12, where he warns of "the spiritual forces of wickedness in the heavenly places." During the present age, he and his demon host dominate, pressure, and control every person who is unsaved. He is the personification of spiritual death because he is the personification of rebellion against God—and so is the system he designed.

Satan is the *archon*, **the prince** and ruler over this world system, and he has placed princes upon every region, town, city, and country with an evil agenda. Not all unsaved people are necessarily indwelt at all times by Satan or are demon–possessed. But knowingly or unknowingly they are subject to Satan's influence. Because they share his nature of sinfulness and exist in the same sphere of rebellion against God, they respond naturally to his leading and to the influence of his demons. They are on the same spiritual wavelength.

It goes to say that you can aim to do good but fail because your flesh was not meant to defeat fleshly things but entice them. It is by the mercy of God by indwelling us in our hearts by His Holy Spirit and by empowering us to fight the flesh. It is the spirit of God that quickens us and strengthens us in times like these. Satan influences media outlets, music, fashion, education, politics, economy, and much more. By the mighty spirit of discernment of God, we can know when and how to move in making decisions when we are embarking on just anything. Anything that is not under the blood of Jesus will bring destruction to our lives.

As with the **world**, the **air** over which Satan has controlling **power** represents the sphere where demons move.

Men are not free and independent; they are totally dominated by the hosts of hell. It is by God's grace through faith that we conquer. It is by the blood of the lamb!

Besides the well-known thought of Satan being thrown out of the presence of God, the war is in heaven. Clearly, there is more than one heaven. Apostle Paul being caught up in the third heaven, it can be justified that we also heaven first and second heaven.

I have written a lot about the subject of having three heavens. Believers who are seated with Christ in the heavenly places are in the third heaven since Christ's throne is there. There is also another thought that says there are seven heavens, however, it is unbiblical. Islam is rooted in the idea of the seventh heavens. As the children of the light, we have to stick to the scriptures and to what the word of God is saying. And also not neglecting the spirit of truth—the Holy Spirit as our guide.

There could be millions of clouds, or billions of planets, or stars, but there are three heavens. As a prophetic individual who has had intense prophetic dreams and visions about the heavens, especially the third heaven, it is confirmation that the Word of God is true. I had an intense out-of-body experience at one point after being discharged from the hospital for a strange ailment that was moving in my stomach. The night I came back, I saw principalities and powers of darkness fighting for my soul in the mid heaven and I saw the hand of God taking me to his presence.

This was the time when I had so many out-of-body experiences. I spent the whole two years suffering from strange evil things moving in my stomach, and something that seemed like a snake in my stomach was moving all over, and at times I felt like the thing wanted to come out of my mouth. I was afraid. My life was going south. But I never lost hope in the Lord God Almighty. Thank God I am still here. And I have grown in the Lord.

Some tests in life are meant to lift you up. Even if sometimes you receive backlash from your friends and family for your faith. God has his own ways of moving in our lives. God's ways are not man's ways. The shaking of the move of God will even disturb your friends and family. People you wholeheartedly trust will turn against you. I am saying this from a prophetic perspective. Many in our families serve the different God or different Jesus we serve.

When you are dealing with principalities and powers of darkness, you are contending with ancient powers that have been influencing the world for ages. Mainly the political landscape of countries and cultural societies overall. Some things that seem to be the norm in our societies are from the Devil. The enemy has also infiltrated the church of Christ. The division and theological differences are the results of demonic and Satanic influence in the churches.

Let me tell you, God is restoring and making a re-arrangement for the bride. The church of Christ is going back to its axis. There is restoration happening in the realm of spirit that shall manifest soon. But it will start in Israel. Bear in mind that, Israel is the pillar and cornerstone of all world churches. Israel is the vine tree. And all are just branches.

We cannot talk about the end times and not talk about Israel. We as Christians make mistakes by taking the Word while neglecting the Jewish history of Jesus Christ. When the time comes when the body of Christ and Jewishness come together in harmony, the veil of the mysteries of the gospel and the Word will be a thing of the past.

This chapter was inspired by Derek Prince's book called War in Heaven. And I have realized that this is what has been going on in the body of Christ. There are evil forces of powers that are in control of our planet Earth. Don't get it wrong, God is all-powerful and all-in-control. However, it is the church that can make the heaven invade the earth. It is all about winning territory. Nowadays men are no longer winning souls like back in the day. Now everyone is all about laying low in their business.

As it was in the days of Noah, so shall the tsunami move of God take over the whole world. Prayer is the accelerator of the move of God which is the move of the spirit, along with signs, wonders, and miracles.

Elites and prestigious people in high power of politics and business are already ushering the beast to come. The beast has not come yet. But the spirit of anti-Christ is already in the system of our society. Many are mocking Christ. Many are denying the faith. Christ is being crucified in politics, media, music, entertainment, and many more. Brethren, when you see the Christian faith being mocked in all four corners of the globe, just know you are on the right track.

You will never hear the media speaking ill about Islam. It is only in Christianity because of the virtues the Christian religion stands for. It is merciful, loving, and forgiving. This is the picture Christ painted while on the cross. And it will still be the same cross that will unite brothers and sisters all over the world to come to the home of love.

Principalities and powers of the air are against this move of God. As much as God wants us to be saved and delivered from the hand of the evil One, the world is painting the picture as if God is evil and Satan is good. Artists have the power to tap into the minds of people through art forms. Thus secular music is the weapon used to control the minds of many people around the nation. We slack on the things that do matter but excel on the things that don't. One would rather spend 10 hours on Tik Tok than 10 minutes on prayer.

We haven't seen technology yet, there is more technology to come in this life and in the ages to come. But it will bring destruction to humanity. It would be like when kids play with matchboxes, and burning will be the result. And this technology comes from another dimension. Mostly it originates from the marine kingdom. I have written a lot about this kingdom. I strongly believe if God wants to use you mighty, he will teach you a lot about the kingdom of darkness.

Any man of God who does know about the kingdom of darkness is bound to suffer defeat. As the minister of the Most High God, you will see demons more than you see angels. Eyes that are opened spiritually, do not only see light but also darkness. It goes to say you can only defeat what you know.

Marine powers work hand in hand with powers from the sky. The Bible clearly says that Satan is the prince of the power of the air. He is a prince in the realm of spirit. only a prince can defeat a prince. Christ is the prince of peace. Peace is above all things.

Prayer against evil powers in the heavenliest (Prayer taken from *Prayers that Rout Demons*)

I am sitting in heavenly places in Christ, far above all

principality, power, might, and dominion (Eph. 1:3).
I take my position in the heavens and bind the principalities
and powers that operate against my life in the name of Jesus.
I break and rebuke every program in the heavens
that would operate against me through the sun,
the moon, the stars, and the constellations.
I bind and rebuke any ungodly forces operating against me
through Arcturus, Pleiades, Mazzaroth, and Orion (Job
38:31–32).
I bind and rebuke all moon deities and demons operating
through the moon in the name of Jesus (2 Kings 23:5).
I bind all sun deities and demons operating through
the sun in the name of Jesus (2 Kings 23:5).
I bind all deities and demons operating through the stars
and planets in the name of Jesus (2 Kings 23:5).
The sun shall not smite me by day nor the moon by night (Ps.
121:6).
The heavens were created to be a blessing to my life.
I receive the rain and blessing from heaven
upon my life in the name of Jesus.
I pray for angels to be released to war against any spirit in the
heavens
assigned to block my prayers from being answered (Dan.
10:12–13).
I bind the prince of the power of the air
in the name of Jesus (Eph. 2:2).
I pray for the floodgates of heaven to be
opened over my life (Mal. 3:10).
I pray for an open heaven, and I bind any demonic
interference from the heavens in the name of Jesus.

Let the evil powers of heaven be shaken in
the name of Jesus (Matt. 24:29).
Let the heavens drop dew upon my life (Deut. 33:28).
Bow the heavens and come down, O Lord (Ps. 144:5).
Let the heavens be opened over my life,
and let me see visions (Ezek. 1:1)
Shake the heavens and fill my house with Your glory (Hag.
2:6–7).
Thunder in the heavens against the enemy, O Lord (Ps.
18:13).
Let the heavens drop at the presence of God (Ps. 68:8).
Let the heavens praise Thy wonders, O Lord (Ps. 89:5).
Show Your wonders in the heavens (Joel 2:30).
Ride upon the heavens and release Your voice, O Lord (Ps.
68:33).
Release Your manifold wisdom to the
powers in the heavens (Eph. 3:10).

The life we live is like we are in the movie whereby we are the good guys as Christians and the bad guys are on the other side waging war with us—more like an intense battle between the protagonist and antagonist. The authority that Satan stripped Adam in the Garden of Eden is restored. Christ is the triumphant lion that defeated the whole kingdom of darkness.

One preacher and teacher I will always cherish his teaching is Derek Prince who once said "The tiny blood of Jesus Christ could destroy the whole kingdom of darkness to the ground". It can only take the prince of peace to destroy the prince of wrath—the Devil. Walking in the power of the gospel of Christ is walking in authority over the wiles of the enemy. The apostles had to be empowered before they could take over the world with the eternal gospel of Christ.

Because the gospel of demons is also the gospel of power. The agents of Satan, witches, wizards, sorcerers, necromancers, enchanters, and the like, are immersed with satanic powers—walking with a bunch of demonic entities to take over territories. It has always been about taking over territories.

I heard the voice of God one time about the heaven invasion over territory. Already principalities and powers of darkness are hovering over communities and societies in every way. The design of God is when the inferred power and authority over the body of Christ is used to influence nations by taking off the blinders and cracking and destroying evil web over the atmosphere limiting the prayers of saints.

If your eyes could open in spirit and see beyond the curtain of clouds, there are dark clouds thicker and harder like steel that you need to destroy for ascension in the realm of spirit. sometimes you will be praying but feeling like you are not doing anything. There are strongmen and powers of evil blocking the prayers of saints to ascend unto God. The same way God smelled the sweet aroma of Noah's sacrifice after the floods, it is the same way when we worship and praise God feels. It is the power of spiritual worship of truth that will change the atmosphere of nations.

Angels must ascend and descend, for the veil has been broken. Christ is that ladder of Jacob that connects the heavens and Earth. The blood of Christ has reconciled all things unto God. This paves a gateway in spirit that the tsunami moves of spirit that we experience, it is through the obedience of this man to the cross—Jesus Christ.

The earthly battle consists of demons. We are not fighting a fleshy fight with humans but with evil powers that a pulling strings in the shadows. And to conquer this battle, you have to be in the shadow of the Almighty God. Victory comes from God. Salvation comes from God.

We have to tap into the power of God through fellowshipping with His Spirit. The spirit of God must be above our flesh. There is enormous grace and power of the spirit when you deny your flesh. Miracles, signs, and wonders come as the result of one denying his or her own flesh to the core.

Back in the day preachers used to tell folks to carry the cross, or to follow the cross. They knew that this was the secret to victory over many challenges befalling us. The more we are like Christ, the more we will do like Christ, act like Christ, talk like Christ, and live like Him. Christ is the perfect example we have here. For a long haul we have been following the world, celebrities, politicians, musicians, and athletics, it is time the table turns.

God is life. And life is in God. The redemption of God is eternal. People may help you here and there, but they do not know what tomorrow holds. Thus, folks, we have to keep our eyes upwards where the throne of God is. Where your eyes are, is where your treasure is. The battle is on, but the recipe is still the holiness of character. Show me the men of great powers, and I will tell you about character.

I tell you the truth, we lose so many battles against Satan as the body of Christ due to unperfected character. Having the holy spirit of God in you has to come to terms with character development. When men like Moses and Samuel spoke, men listened and demons trembled. None of Samuel's prophecies fell to the ground. God fulfilled every word prophet Samuel spoke. Because these were holy men who feared God. Our generation is filled with the idea that God is love that we end up sinning deliberately knowing that God is love and He will forgive. While it is true, it is also true that God is holy. And He hates sin. However, He loves the sinner with an unconditional love.

The battle within

Dear Believer, you may have heard the saying, "The battle is within." These words hold profound truth for anyone who seeks to walk in faith. While we often think of spiritual warfare as external battles against forces beyond us, it's crucial to recognize that the most significant battle is often fought within ourselves.

As a believer, understanding this internal struggle and how to overcome it is essential for your spiritual growth and well-being. Apostle Paul talked about the scales blinding the believers to receive the gospel of Christ. These are evil powers of the air that a territorial within society and stand as the gatekeepers denying believers the salvation of God. The main of the enemy is to have as many people as possible missing going to heaven.

We teach more about spiritual warfare because we are at war already. It is within the nature of every being to go through spiritual attacks. It does not matter whether you are strong or weak, we go through attacks from the camp of the enemy. Every believer taking a stand in faith will likely go through a rough patch in life. But God will safeguard our lives. Christian living is an adventurous journey of the unknown—though we know that He is with us through storms.

He will cover you with spirit of heaviness limiting you the joy of the Lord. When all things in your life go south, you are stressed and you cannot think straight. The enemy wants this: believers with wavering faith in Jesus Christ.

My brothers and sisters, the spirit of God will never fail us. I have noticed that lately, the attacks of the enemy have been coming from all directions, media, music, movies, and books have been the pinpoint of attacks on humanity lately.

There are some movies that I have watched and felt like the film was initiating me. Many of the visions or dreams we see after watching these kinds of films are demonic. When your mind is renewed through the Word of God, you flee from anything that does not glorify Jesus Christ. If the Almighty God is not the center of pleasure, then the enemy is the center. Many do not need deliverance prayers, they just need to distance themselves from certain places, people, music, movies, and the like.

I am not saying all music is bad but we all know that the majority of them do not glorify God. Mind control is big in this industry. They offer you a service that you will never forget. I am sure any of you have experienced this when you love a song too much you will sometimes find it playing in your subconscious mind even when you are asleep. You will hear the tune of that song from afar in your mind.

These musician' chants spell over their song to reach masses even in distant lands. Many have even sold out to the Devil. You are literally in the Devil's courtyard if you are into these kinds of music. It is not only music but the whole entertainment industry is rigged by principal demons. Ancients' fallen spirits like Baphomet, Moloch, Baal, and Ashtoreth are ruling the entertainment game period.

These are the external sources that distract us from walking in perfection with God. The battle within is the battle of the mind. The mind of a born-again believer is to be daily renewed with the Word of God. Salvation brings righteousness However, it is your ability and responsibility to walk in holiness. Being holy means you are different and set apart from the world.

The secret to victory in all spiritual attacks is to stand on the truth of Ephesians 12, knowing and acknowledging that we are dealing with spirits, not humans. And the fight requires spiritual weapons: authority in the name of Jesus, applying and pleading the blood of Jesus, praise as a weapon, and many more.

I have written a lot about the weapons of warfare. Check out my specific book on this subject called *Weapons of Warfare Against The Wiles of The Devil.*

As someone who has come in contact with regional and territorial spirits in my hometown, the most important thing you have to protect is your mind. If evil powers can infiltrate your mind, your faith is bound to be shaken. Faith is above all things. Through your faith, you got your salvation. Through faith, you are able to defeat the wiles of the enemy.

The enemy will target your mind to shake your faith. All these different emotions that you feel when things are not going your way are usually small stepping stones for him to beat you so that you give up on the Lord.

Your inner battle is not a sign of weakness; rather, it's evidence that you have embarked on a spiritual journey. The enemy often attacks from within, sowing seeds of doubt, temptation, and guilt. Recognizing this inner struggle is the first step toward victory.

Scriptural Guidance

The King James Bible provides profound wisdom and guidance on how to overcome the battle within. In Ephesians 6:12 (KJV), Paul says, "For we wrestle not against flesh and blood, but against principalities, against powers, against the rulers of the darkness of this world, against spiritual wickedness in high places." This verse reminds us that our battle is not physical but spiritual.

To overcome this spiritual warfare within, consider these scriptural principles:

Put on the Armor of God

In Ephesians 6:13-17 (KJV), Paul instructs believers to put on the whole armor of God, including the belt of truth, the breastplate of righteousness, the shield of faith, the helmet of salvation, and the sword of the Spirit. These elements represent spiritual attributes and practices that protect and empower you in your internal battle.

Renew Your Mind

In Romans 12:2 (KJV), Paul advises, "And be not conformed to this world: but be ye transformed by the renewing of your mind." The battle within often begins in the mind. To overcome it, fill your thoughts with God's Word, meditate on His promises, and reject negative and sinful thinking patterns.

Walk in the Spirit

Galatians 5:16 (KJV) says, "This I say then, Walk in the Spirit, and ye shall not fulfil the lust of the flesh." To win the battle within, cultivate a close relationship with the Holy Spirit. Seek His guidance, rely on His strength, and allow Him to lead your life.

Confess and Repent

In 1 John 1:9 (KJV), we are reminded, "If we confess our sins, he is faithful and just to forgive us our sins, and to cleanse us from all unrighteousness." When you stumble in your internal battle, don't hesitate to confess your sins and seek forgiveness. Repentance is a powerful weapon against the enemy.

Seek Fellowship

Hebrews 10:25 (KJV) encourages us, "Not forsaking the assembling of ourselves together, as the manner of some is; but exhorting one another." Engaging in fellowship with other believers provides mutual support, encouragement, and accountability in your battle within.

The battle within is real, but so is your capacity to overcome it. As a believer, you are equipped with the Word of God and the Holy Spirit to navigate this internal struggle victoriously. Remember the words of 1 John 4:4 (KJV), "Ye are of God, little children, and have overcome them: because greater is he that is in you, than he that is in the world."

By putting on the armor of God, renewing your mind, walking in the Spirit, confessing and repenting, and seeking fellowship, you can conquer the battle within. Trust in the promises of the King James Bible and lean on your faith to guide you through this spiritual warfare within.

May you find strength, peace, and victory in your journey of faith.

Healing and Deliverance from Territorial Spiritual Attacks

In the realm of spiritual warfare, one often encounters a distinct type of challenge: territorial spiritual attacks. These attacks are focused on specific geographic areas, regions, or communities. While they may manifest in various forms, the effects can be profound, affecting not only individuals but entire communities. This chapter explores the concept of territorial spiritual attacks and how believers can seek healing and deliverance from them, drawing upon scriptural references and spiritual insights.

Understanding Territorial Spiritual Attacks

You will often wonder why certain things repeat themselves within the society or community. In my community, a month will not pass without breaking news of someone committing suicide by hanging themselves. Youths are taking themselves out like their lives are meaningless. It pains me the most because many go on social media to bid goodbyes before killing themselves.

This is a territorial issue. In fact, it is happening around the globe. When someone feels like things are not going as planned, they see death as the only way out. I am sure you also have things in your community that repeat itself as a pattern. Also, the other thing that keeps many under pressure is social media. When they see their friends depicting a certain lifestyle as if they are prospering, that puts many under pressure to get things together.

Unfortunately, if it does not go according to plan—we witness disaster everywhere. We have to learn to trust the process and to put God first in all things. He blesses and rewards abundantly those who trust in Him. Trusting in God is having faith in His unwavering promises found in the holy scriptures.

The Scriptural Foundation

The Bible contains several instances that provide insight into the existence of territorial spirits and the need for healing and deliverance. In the Old Testament, we find references to territorial entities like the "prince of Persia" in the book of Daniel (Daniel 10:13) and the "rulers of darkness" in Ephesians 6:12. These passages suggest that spiritual forces can have dominion over regions.

Seeking Healing and Deliverance

Believers facing territorial spiritual attacks should approach the situation with faith, prayer, and spiritual discernment. Here are some steps to consider:

1. Acknowledge the Spiritual Reality: Recognize that territorial spiritual attacks are a genuine aspect of spiritual warfare. Acknowledging their existence is the first step towards healing and deliverance.

2. Seek Spiritual Guidance: Consult with spiritual leaders, mentors, or pastors who can provide insight and support. They can help you discern the nature of the attack and offer guidance on how to address it.

3. Prayer and Fasting: Engage in focused prayer and fasting. In Matthew 17:21 (KJV), Jesus said, "Howbeit this kind goeth not out but by prayer and fasting." This demonstrates the power of these spiritual disciplines in overcoming strongholds.

4. Spiritual Warfare Prayers: Utilize specific prayers designed for spiritual warfare and territorial deliverance. These prayers often include renouncing the influence of dark forces and claiming the authority of Christ.

5. Scripture-Based Declarations: Speak and declare scripture verses that emphasize God's authority and sovereignty over all realms. For example, Psalm 24:1 (KJV) states, "The earth is the Lord's, and the fulness thereof; the world, and they that dwell therein."

6. Unity in Prayer: Join together with other believers in your community to pray collectively against the territorial attacks. Matthew 18:20 (KJV) assures us, "For where two or three are gathered together in my name, there am I in the midst of them."

7. Spiritual Cleansing: Engage in spiritual cleansing rituals, such as anointing your home with consecrated oil or dedicating your living space to God's protection.

8. Perseverance: Understand that deliverance from territorial spiritual attacks may not be immediate. Maintain a steadfast and persistent prayer life, trusting in God's timing.

Conclusion

Territorial spiritual attacks are a complex aspect of spiritual warfare that requires a deep understanding of the spiritual realm and a reliance on God's power and authority. While these attacks may be formidable, believers have the tools and resources to seek healing and deliverance. Through prayer, fasting, scripture, and unity in faith, individuals and communities can overcome the influence of malevolent forces and reclaim their territories for the glory of God.

As you face territorial spiritual attacks, remember the words of 1 John 4:4 (KJV): "Ye are of God, little children, and have overcome them: because greater is he that is in you than he that is in the world." With faith and perseverance, you can experience healing and deliverance from these challenges, bringing light and hope to your region.

God made the heavens and earth. He found the dry land out of the floods. Water makes up 70% of our lives. We cannot survive without water. The water realm has some of the deep mysteries that haven't even this world tapped in. From the moment of our birth, we are intimately connected to water. It sustains our bodies, nourishes the earth, and carries a spiritual symbolism that permeates cultures and faiths around the world.

Let's dive into the depths of this mysterious element and explore its spiritual significance. I have always known the water realm as a portal to another dimension. When a woman is about to give birth, the water breaks, and then she gives forth what she has been carrying. Women's bodies are portals of the carriers of the glory of God.

By the way, the throne of God in the heavenly places is found upon water. Water is also the symbol of the movement of the spirit of God. Satan knew about the power of water. He used to be in the presence of God walking in perfection knowing all kinds of wisdom. This is written in Isaiah 14 and Ezekiel 28.

Since he knows that God's throne is upon the waters. He also has his kingdom in the sea ruling humankind bringing all hell and destruction upon humanity. He is the guy who wanted to be like the Most High and have His throne above the stars.

The old teachings used to tell us that Satan rules and lives in hell. How can someone who lives in hell have so much control over every aspect of our lives? And this teaching does not have a scriptural foundation. I wish it was true that Satan is in hell, but no, he is not. He is the prince of the power of the air. He is up there in the second heaven. He also has access to the third heaven where he accuses us daily before the Living God. We are no different than Job and the High Priest Joshua—these men were accused by Satan before the throne of Almighty God.

As much as there is beauty in the kingdom of God, the kingdom of darkness also follows the same pattern of God in structure and order. But they are doing the opposite of what God is doing.

The Lord has been revealing so much about the kingdom of darkness that is situated in the heavenly. My Christian believers are still rooted in the ideology that Satan rules in hell. The lake of fire is his final destination and with his fallen angels and demons. The book of Enoch and Revelation talks about this.

However, he has three kingdoms; in the second heaven, he has strongholds—caging angelic beings who are sent by Almighty God on a mission to planet Earth. This is what happened to Angel Gabriel while coming to Prophet Daniel with answers. The delayed breakthroughs and blessings we suffer might be because of these evil forces in high places. It is vital that when we pray we ask God to strengthen the Angelic powers in our lives so that we see breakthroughs.

Since we are in the end days, Archangel Michael must arise for there is too much chaos in this life. Satan knows that His time is up, therefore, unleashing dangerous forces to keep many stagnant and backward in their walk with God.

The moment you sense that your prayer life has gone south instead of north, it is time to pull up your socks. Prayer and fasting can do serious damage to the kingdom of darkness if it is done in line with the scriptures. Isaiah 58 has a whole chapter about the principle and power of fasting. There is power in the fasted life. Ancient believers knew about the power of denying the flesh through fasting and praying. It is an act of humility and God exalts them that humble themselves.

The purpose of the Marine Kingdom

The purpose of this kingdom is to enslave men. Many people and believers in general are walking in shame because of stolen destiny. Many celebrities confess to selling their soul to the Devil in exchange for fame, riches, and power, and think that Satan has riches and wealth while are stolen virtues from sons of men.

The cornerstone of the kingdom of darkness is stealing, killing, and destroying human beings. While Satan was tempting Christ on the mountain with the riches of the world, he was basically advertising what he had been stealing from man since the beginning of this world.

His plan was to pervert sexuality—opposing the perfect plan of God from the start. Throughout the ages, men and women have fallen because of sexual immorality. There is nothing wrong with a godly sexual encounter that will always align with the perfect will of God which is a godly marriage between men and women.

Marine powers are rooted in ungodly sex. Some agents of the marine kingdom are assigned on the mission to destroy through sex. We all know that sex is power and that sex is spiritual. They capitalize on the fact that men are weak when it comes to sexual pleasure. Many have fallen like Babylon through sexual encounters with ladies initiated in the marine kingdom.

Once this kingdom can capture your semen, your life will be manipulated to the ground. You will bound to fall, businesses, careers, marriage, and your prayer life will go down south indeed. Sex is a dangerous weapon when is done outside the will of God.

There is this pastor who I know in my hometown village who went on to acquire powers from the marine kingdom so that he can display prophetic and healing powers in his church. He was the talk of the town demonstrating powers many thought were coming from God. Unbeknown they were coming from the kingdom of darkness. Majority of these prophetic individuals who will prophesy your place, your ID number, phone number, and many other silly things, are not to be trusted.

The true prophets of God moved nations to repentance. Prophets like Samuel had so much audacity in the walk and in their talk that villages would tremble when they saw him and enquired if he came in peace or if the Lord had something against them. Same with the general of Israel, Elijah, these men were moved by the spirit of God to change the curtains of their nations to the ordinances and oracles of God.

It's funny that some will even go as far as telling you the color of your underwear. What has this got to do with the gospel of Christ? The man was in like manner. Deceiving the church with his silly prophetic gimmicks and magic from the Marine

Kingdom. You will actually think you are being healed and delivered when you are in their churches while you are being initiated into their kingdom without you realizing it.

This cult allows the pastor to sleep with his women and his children as well. Many around the world have these calibers of prophetic individuals and overall religious leaders who went through the easy route of demonic deception of false power and fame to display in churches. If you do not walk in the spirit of discernment you will be the victim of demonic manipulation. Sadly, it takes a long haul to disconnect yourself from the altars of these so-called religious leaders.

I am not condemning the body of Christ; I am sharing with you the reality of what we are up to. As much as we can make up thousands in membership in our respective churches, not all are on fire for the move of God. And not all are for Christ.

I am letting you know that there is nothing good that can come from the kingdom of darkness. It is only the light of God that will liberate many souls from destruction. Deliverance comes from the God of our salvation who will always bring us close to Him through the redemption blood of Christ.

Water is 70 percent in man's body, and also in Earth, water covers 70 percent. Thereby the Marine Kingdom is extensive and has its tentacles in each city, town, and village. From lakes, rivers, wells, springs, dams, and oceans, the Marine Kingdom has and is still effective in its functions. The marine Kingdom tends to be controlling of all that is marine-connected. From Food, Communication, Life, Clothing, Industries, Power Centre's, Building and others.

This marine Kingdom has recently grown strong and is recruiting a lot of innocent folks without their notice. As it's the End times, the Devil's falling is primarily upon two Habitations of men: Earth and Seas.

Their purpose is to kill, steal, and destroy. The destinies of great men and women of God are caged in the water. Many souls have been manipulated and exchanged without their knowledge. Marine spirits like maneuvering through dreams to sleep with their victim to steal their glory and power. The Devil will steal your power and control you with your own power. Be sober and alert at all times.

The effect of the marine kingdom

You know how the game plays out when you have been messing with the wrong people—bitter results. Not positive! This is the same when you are being attacked by the marine demons and agents. Rivers, streams, dams, and oceans near your village, town, or city happen to be the portals of many marine kingdoms. The marine kingdom is a government on its own.

I have seen the Devil's throne under the sea through dreams and visions. It's the city underwater where there are activities and meetings going on. They will recruit anyone who is willing to work hard in turning this world into a satanic worship.

Water is a mystery. You cannot function at your best if you do not drink water as you should. Doctors recommend a certain consumption a day. We use water almost every day of our lives. It is a great mystery why Satan has infiltrated the water realm in order to control humanity. Many of our ancestors were formed into venerating water deities. Many believers are struggling to part ways with the marine kingdom. It is a long and intense journey of deliverance from these marine spirits.

Some things go out not except through prayer and fasting. I have seen tremendous breakthroughs through prayer and fasting. Denying your flesh elevates your spirit man to wage war against the wiles of the Devil. In fact, miracles, signs, and wonders are the results of us denying the flesh to raise our spirit into the higher realm in Christ. There is always a ladder to climb in this kingdom of God. Apostle John was called to come up high, and he saw serious visions that we still talking about today. The book of Revelation came as John allowed the spirit of God to move in his life. Where the spirit of God is, there is liberty.

Effects of Marine Kingdom (Water Spirits) in the Life of Believers:

- **Spiritual Oppression:** Believers may experience spiritual oppression, such as nightmares, sleep disturbances, and a sense of spiritual heaviness, caused by marine spirits.
- **Stagnation:** These spirits can hinder personal and spiritual growth, leading to a sense of being stuck or unfulfilled in life.
- **Emotional Turmoil:** Emotional instability, mood swings, and unexplained sadness or anxiety can result from the influence of marine spirits.
- **Financial Challenges:** Believers may face financial difficulties, including unexpected financial losses, debt, and lack of prosperity.
- **Relationship Problems:** Strained or broken

relationships, particularly in marriages or partnerships, may occur due to the interference of marine spirits.

- **Health Issues:** Some believers attribute unexplained health problems to the influence of marine spirits, although it's important to seek medical advice for health concerns.
- **Barrenness and Infertility:** Struggles with fertility or barrenness may be associated with the activities of marine spirits.

How to Overcome Marine Demons:

- **Prayer and Fasting:** Engage in focused prayer and fasting to seek divine intervention and protection from marine spirits.
- **Renounce and Repent:** Renounce any known or unknown connections with the marine kingdom, and repent for any involvement with occult practices or sin.
- **Use of Scripture:** Utilize relevant scripture verses, such as Psalm 18:44-45, to declare victory over marine spirits.
- **Seek Deliverance Ministries:** Seek assistance from reputable deliverance ministries or pastors experienced in spiritual warfare for guidance and prayers.
- **Holy Water and Anointing Oil:** Use holy water and anointing oil, often blessed by a spiritual leader, for

cleansing and protection.

- **Spiritual Discernment:** Develop spiritual discernment to recognize the presence and activities of marine spirits in your life.
- **Strengthen Your Faith:** Build a strong foundation of faith in God and His power to overcome spiritual opposition.
- **Fellowship and Support:** Seek support from fellow believers and engage in group prayer and worship for added spiritual strength.
- **Consistent Spiritual Growth:** Focus on consistent spiritual growth through reading the Bible, attending church, and maintaining a close relationship with God.
- **Maintain Moral and Ethical Living:** Live a life of moral and ethical integrity, avoiding sin and practices that may open doors to spiritual attacks.

It's important to approach these matters with caution and discernment, seeking guidance from spiritual leaders and maintaining a balanced perspective on spiritual warfare. Not all challenges in life are necessarily attributed to the influence of marine spirits, and it's essential to seek professional help when facing serious emotional or health issues.

Power against Marine spirits

Through Christ we conquer, and we shall conquer until the end of time. It is the anointing that breaks the yoke of the Devil. The oil of God shall bring gladness upon our faces. As Moses delivered the Israelites by the mighty hand of God, you shall also be delivered from sicknesses, incurable diseases whereby doctors see nothing, the spirit of God searches all things.

And whatever you desire and needs, comes from this spirit. Jesus did not leave the church powerless, but with the mighty spirit of God—preceding from the very throne of God!

The following are the Demonic signs to MARINE SPIRITS:

– Barrenness Sometimes Is Associated with It.

– Chronic Masturbation.

– Dreams of Swimming in Rivers or Oceans.

– Dreams of Having Sex with known or unknown people are connected to Marine spirits.

– Dream of Playing with snakes and the presence of frogs in one's dream.

– Sudden and Mysterious missing personal effects like Undergarments.

– Excessive Pride — Uncontrollable Anger and Outbursts.

– Suicidal Thoughts and Dreams of being killed.

– Fear of Water, i.e. rivers, lakes, oceans.

– Constant Smell That's Irritating Even After Bathing.

– Wearing of Ornaments from Unknown Sources.

– Getting Mysterious Objects at Your House, Room, Or even mysterious letters.

– Been initiated through unholy Sex, fornication, or sex with agents.

– Bedwetting Is clear and also associated with the spirit of Immaturity and stagnation.

– Chronic Spinsterhood and Chronic Bachelorhood.

– Excessive Urge of Sex Without Control.

– Excessive Lust.

– Dreams of Receiving Money from a very Beautiful Woman or Man

– Breaking of Other people's marriage and being without remorse.

– A Youthful Man or Woman, unmarried and yet Desires Married Men or Women.

– Marine Kingdom is the Number one Promoter of Polygamy.

– Addicted to Music Ungodly Music.

– Dreams of Been Given Excess Wealth from Unknown Sources in Return of Favors.

Prayers Against Marine evil powers

No weapon formed against me shall prosper in the mighty name of Jesus.

No weapon from the marine world shall shutter my dreams in the name of Jesus.

The mighty hand of God is upon me to silence every demon of the water in the name of Jesus.

I have authority and power over the powers of darkness in the mighty name of Jesus.

Every altar of the queen seated in the water, be destroyed to the ground by fire in the mighty name of Jesus.

Evil marine priest assigned to destroy and cage my destiny under the sea, be destroyed in the fire of God of Elijah.

God of Elijah arise and scatter my enemies with your mighty wind.

Let your north wind scatter every altar that is speaking ill against me in the mighty name of Jesus.

Blood of Jesus destroys every marine altar over my body in the name of Jesus.

I speak the fall of every evil altar that is on fire for my career, finance, ministry, and marriage in the mighty name of Jesus.

The mighty fire of God surrounds me and my family in the name of Jesus.

Every marine seed in my body, be destroyed by the fire of the holy fire of God.

From head to toe, I am covered with the blood of Jesus.

My eyes are covered with the countenance of God.

My ears are covered with the blood of Jesus.

My feet are covered with the blood of Jesus.

Every snake spirit rapped itself over my genitals, be destroyed by the holy ghost fire.

Fire over every object on my body that does not come from God.

Anything that does not come from God in my life, be removed in the mighty name of Jesus.

I am strong in the Lord and in the power of His might in Christ.

I am seated in the heavenly places in Christ.

I am far above marine powers in the mighty name of Jesus.

Every mermaid or merman spirit that is sleeping with me in my dreams, catch fire in the mighty name of Jesus.

Every marine covenant be broken in the name of Jesus.

Every marine contract be destroyed in the mighty name of Jesus.

Every agent of the marine initiating me through evil spiritual food be destroyed by the blood of Jesus.

F asting
Matthew 6:16-18 (NIV):

"When you fast, do not look somber as the hypocrites do, for they disfigure their faces to show others they are fasting. Truly I tell you, they have their reward. But when you fast, put oil on your head and wash your face, so that it will not be obvious to others that you are fasting, but only to your Father, who is unseen; and your Father, who sees what is done in secret, will reward you."

Isaiah 58:6-7 (NIV):

"Is not this the kind of fasting I have chosen: to loose the chains of injustice and untie the cords of the yoke, to set the oppressed free and break every yoke? Is it not to share your food with the hungry and to provide the poor wanderer with shelter—when you see the naked, to clothe them, and not to turn away from your own flesh and blood?"

Joel 2:12 (NIV):

"Even now," declares the Lord, "return to me with all your heart, with fasting and weeping and mourning."

Acts 13:2-3 (NIV):

"While they were worshiping the Lord and fasting, the Holy Spirit said, 'Set apart for me Barnabas and Saul for the work to which I have called them.' So after they had fasted and prayed, they placed their hands on them and sent them off."

Ezra 8:23 (NIV):

"So we fasted and petitioned our God about this, and he answered our prayer."

• • • •

THESE SCRIPTURES HIGHLIGHT the importance of fasting in seeking God's guidance, repentance, and spiritual growth, as well as its role in acts of charity and justice. An act of humility is honored by God. Jesus started his ministry by empowering his spirit man by fasting. Even though in spirit he is a mighty God, he had to afflict his soul by fasting.

Psalm 35:13

13 But as for me, when they were sick, my clothing was sackcloth: I

humbled my soul with fasting; and my prayer returned into mine own bosom.

Fasting empowers your spirit man. It gives the holy spirit room in your body to move without disturbance. Many Christians after prayer and fasting, testify of hearing the voice of God clearly than when they do not. I am also able to discern spirits easily when I fast and my prayer life is dramatically empowered when I humble my soul through fasting.

Besides many adopting a fasted lifestyle to cleanse the body and mind, fasting is a demon slayer. It is written that it is the anointing that breaks the yoke. Jesus Christ returned from the wilderness with spirit and power demonstrating deliverance and healing to many who were afflicted. I would also encourage you to humble your soul through fasting, you shall be exalted.

You shall see amazing results in your finances and health. Though we are not fasting for material things. However, God is the rewarder for all who diligently seek Him. And you will also be able to hear the voice of the holy spirit in a clearer way. Because many fall short of the glory of God in their lives for missing it when the spirit is talking. What many are seeking break-throughs for, have already received answers in dreams and visions.

Folks, never neglect those dreams and visions.

• • • •

JOB 33:14-16 (NIV):

"For God does speak—now one way, now another—though no one perceives it. In a dream, in a vision of the night, when deep sleep falls on people as they slumber in their beds, he may speak in their ears and terrify them with warnings."

When you call upon God, He answers you by showing you through visions and dreams before manifestation. If we had harkened unto the voice of God, many wouldn't be living in miserable marriages and so on. God talks at all times through various means; through dreams, visions, scriptures, intuition, small still voice, trance, through numbers, other believers, prophecy, and more. This is not a closed call. And fasting can open so many channels in which God speaks and experience more and more of His glory.

Mark 9:14-29 tells us about a time when the disciples were unable to cast a demon out of a boy. When Jesus arrived, he cast out the spirit, and the boy was set free and healed. His disciples did not understand why they had the power to do some miracles but not this one, and Jesus told him, "And when He had come into the house, His disciples asked Him privately, "Why could we not cast it out?" So He said to them, "This kind can come out by nothing but prayer and fasting.""

God moves in even greater ways as we fast, pray, and increase our faith.

When the greatness of the problems in the world overwhelms you, it is a call to fast and pray.

When you see the brokenness of the world around you, let the urgency lead you to desperation for God to move. Let it lead you to seek God in a greater way through fasting and prayer.

5 Is it such a fast that I have chosen? a day for a man to afflict his soul? is it
to bow down his head as a bulrush, and to spread sackcloth and ashes under
him? wilt thou call this a fast, and an acceptable day to the
LORD?
6 Is not this the fast that I have chosen? to loose the bands of
wickedness, to
undo the heavy burdens, and to let the oppressed go free, and that ye break every
yoke?
7 Is it not to deal thy bread to the hungry, and that thou bring the poor that
are cast out to thy house? when thou seest the naked, that thou cover him; and
that thou hide not thyself from thine own flesh?
8 Then shall thy light break forth as the morning, and thine health shall
spring forth speedily: and thy righteousness shall go before thee; the glory of the
LORD shall be thy rereward.
9 Then shalt thou call, and the LORD shall answer; thou shalt cry, and he
shall say, Here I am. If thou take away from the midst of thee the yoke, the
putting forth of the finger, and speaking vanity; 10 And if thou draw out thy soul

to the hungry, and satisfy the afflicted soul; then shall thy light
rise in obscurity,
and thy darkness be as the noon day:
11 And the LORD shall guide thee continually, and satisfy
thy soul in
drought, and make fat thy bones: and thou shalt be like a wa-
tered garden, and
like a spring of water, whose waters fail not.
12 And they that shall be of thee shall build the old waste
places: thou shalt raise up the foundations of many genera-
tions; and thou shalt be called, The
repairer of the breach, The restorer of paths to dwell in.

Warfare prayers

We always teach and stress engaging in strategic warfare prayers because of the times we live in. strategic means going by the leading of the spirit of God—the holy spirit. it is child's play when dealing with evil power in heavenly places. Daniel accelerated his prayers through fasting. It took Daniel 21 days to defeat the principalities of the kingdom of Persia. Principal demons are named by the region they inhabit. The fallen spirit may hit the area with witchcraft spirit, death, rejection, poverty, etc. but will identify itself according to the name of the region.

Moses and Joshua during their respective leadership, they have also encountered giants along their journey to the promised land. The giants are still there. Each one of us has giants in closets that are disturbing us from reaching the fullness of the glory of God. Joshua and Caleb defeated their own giants. David destroyed Goliath. Elijah silenced the worship of

Baal and Ashtoreth in Israel. Jehu destroyed Jezebel. What's more, Jesus Christ overcomes Satan and principalities and powers.

We are no longer slaves in this kingdom—we are the friends of God through Christ. We walk in the same anointing of the saints of old. Even better, we have more grace than then because the veil has been torn. We can boldly go to the throne of grace and ask for mercy for all aspects of our lives.

God saw a mighty warrior in Gideon. Gideon saw himself as insignificant to the call of God. You may feel as if God is no longer interested in your prayer, or you may feel worthless because of the sins you have committed, but I tell you, God sees you differently from the way you look at yourself. He sees a mighty warrior in a weak man. He sees a prophet in a person who cannot speak. David went from being a shepherd to a king of Israel.

All these men that I mentioned were warriors in the Lord. In prayer and in deeds. David was a spiritual warfare warrior through his harp. He is the first deliverance minster in the bible who drove out demons through praise and worship.

As we are in the last days, surviving in these seasons will require us to wage spiritual warfare against the wiles of the enemy. The arrows of the Devil fly in the day and night (Psalm 91). Now weapon formed against us shall prosper in the name of Jesus right? Yes, when the holy spirit of God dwells in you, no weapon formed against you shall prosper.

The church should know how to wage spiritual warfare and pray warfare prayers against the enemy. Satan hates the church, that's why there is division, conflict, and animosity among leadership and membership. A house that is divided cannot be blessed by the hand of the Most High God.

We are not fighting people with flesh but the spiritual powers of wickedness that plant these evil seeds within the hearts of faithful people. When men sleep, He plants evil trees in the garden. As the body of Christ, we should not sleep but be the watchmen of the glory of Christ. This can happen when we learn about the weapons of warfare that the Lord God has entrusted the church with.

Midnight warfare engaging

You cannot deny the power of praying at midnight especially if you are always under constant attacks. The time between 12 PM-3 AM is crucial for your breakthrough. This is the time Moses led the Israelites out of Egypt by the mighty hand of God. This is the time when Gideon demolished the altars of his forefathers, the altar of Baal. I am not saying this is the only time you can pray; you can pray anytime. However, through experience and through intense study of the Word of God, midnight prayers are potent weapons against the powers of darkness.

And the kingdom of darkness thrives at these hours. The agents of Satan do not sleep at all, when men are asleep, they are planting demonic seeds. This is the time when you should be up all night uprooting every tree that the Father did not plant in your life. Making declarations and decrees in accordance with the Word of God against the evil powers holding us in cages. The Devil is a liar!

Engaging in midnight prayer warfare against the wiles of the enemy can be a powerful and spiritually enriching practice. Here are some practical steps to help you effectively engage in midnight prayer warfare:

1. **Set Your Intention:** Begin by setting a clear intention for your midnight prayer warfare. Understand what specific spiritual battle you are facing or what area of your life needs divine intervention.

2. **Fasting (Optional):** Fasting can intensify your focus and spiritual sensitivity during midnight prayer. Consult with your spiritual leader or mentor for guidance on fasting, especially if you have any health concerns.

3. **Choose a Quiet Place:** Find a quiet and secluded place where you won't be disturbed during your midnight prayer. This creates an environment conducive to deep spiritual concentration.

4. **Prepare Your Heart:** Before you start praying, take some time to prepare your heart. Repent of any known sins and seek forgiveness from God. Approach Him with humility and a contrite spirit.

5. **Praise and Worship:** Begin your midnight prayer with praise and worship. Sing hymns, songs, or simply offer heartfelt praise to God for His greatness, goodness, and power.

6. **Scripture and Declarations:** Incorporate relevant Bible verses and declarations into your prayer. Use God's Word as a powerful weapon against the enemy's schemes. Scriptures related to spiritual warfare,

protection, and victory are particularly helpful.

7. **Specific Prayer Points:** Identify specific prayer points related to the spiritual battle you are facing. Pray for protection, guidance, wisdom, and the defeat of the enemy's plans. Be specific and persistent in your requests.

8. **Binding and Loosing:** In accordance with Matthew 18:18, you can bind the enemy's activities and loose God's blessings and protection. Declare that no weapon formed against you shall prosper (Isaiah 54:17).

9. **Pray in the Spirit:** If you have the gift of praying in tongues or speaking in a spiritual language, engage in this form of prayer. It can be particularly effective in spiritual warfare (1 Corinthians 14:2, Ephesians 6:18).

10. **Intercession:** Lift up the needs and concerns of others in your prayers. Intercession not only helps others but also strengthens your own spiritual warfare efforts.

11. **Persist in Prayer:** Midnight prayer warfare may require persistence. Jesus encourages us to keep asking, seeking, and knocking (Matthew 7:7-8). Don't be discouraged if you don't see immediate results.

12. **Thanksgiving:** Conclude your prayer session with thanksgiving and praise. Trust that God has heard your prayers and will answer them according to His will.

13. **Spiritual Protection:** After your midnight prayer, ask God for His protection over you, your loved ones, and

your home. Cover yourself with the spiritual armor described in Ephesians 6:10-18.

14. **Maintain Consistency:** Consistency is key in midnight prayer warfare. Establish a routine that works for you, whether it's nightly or at specific intervals, and continue to seek God's guidance.

Remember that midnight prayer warfare is not about relying on your own strength but placing your trust in God's power and sovereignty. As you engage in this spiritual discipline, stay vigilant, stay in God's Word, and seek the support of a spiritual mentor or community for guidance and accountability.

Praise as a weapon

In the epic battle of spiritual warfare against the dark forces, praise and worship emerge as a potent weapon, capable of dismantling the strongholds of territorial spirits, principalities, and powers of darkness. While this concept may seem complex, let's explore it in simple terms, much like a heroic tale where music and songs become a formidable ally against evil.

Praise and Worship: The Musical Armor

Imagine you are a knight preparing to face a fearsome dragon. What if your armor was not made of steel but of beautiful, powerful music? Praise and worship are like that enchanted armor. When we sing, pray, and praise God with our hearts, we put on this musical armor, which shields us from the attacks of darkness.

Territorial Spirits and Powers of Darkness

In the grand story of life, there are good forces (like angels) and bad forces (like demons). Sometimes, bad forces take control over places, causing problems and sadness. These are territorial spirits and powers of darkness. They want to bring fear, hatred, and sadness.

How Praise and Worship Work

Imagine singing a beautiful song that makes you feel happy and safe. When we sing songs and praises to God, it's like we're turning on a powerful light in a dark room. Darkness can't stay where there's light!

So, when we sing and praise God, it's like sending a message to the bad forces: "You can't be here anymore!" They can't stand the light and the happiness that praise and worship bring.

Examples from the Bible

In the Bible, there's a story about a king named Jehoshaphat. When he and his people faced a big army of enemies, they didn't fight with swords but with songs and praise to God. Guess what happened? God confused the enemy armies, and they defeated each other!

Another story is about Paul and Silas. They were in jail, but instead of being sad, they sang praises to God. Suddenly, there was an earthquake, and the jail doors flew open! Their praise broke the chains, and they were free.

Our Musical Battle

In our spiritual battle, praise and worship are our musical weapons. When we sing and praise God, it's like we're sending a powerful message to the bad forces: "You can't win, because God is with us!"

Conclusion

In the great story of life, praise, and worship are our enchanted musical armor against the dark forces. They light up our path, drive away fear and sadness, and remind us that God is always with us. Just like heroes in a tale, we can face any challenge with our musical weapons, knowing that the powers of darkness will never stand a chance against the mighty God we worship and adore. Praise and worship make us victorious in the epic battle of spiritual warfare.

The mystery of binding and loosing

Imagine you have a secret weapon to defeat the bad guys in a video game. Binding and loosing demons in the spiritual realm are a bit like having a superpower against evil powers. This mysterious concept might sound complex, but let's break it down in simple terms that even a primary school kid can understand.

Binding and Loosing: What's That?

Picture this: You have a magical rope that can tie up the bad guys, making them powerless. That's like "binding" in the spiritual world. When we bind demons, we're telling them they can't harm us or others anymore. We're tying them up!

Now, imagine you have a magical key that can unlock doors and set people free. That's like "loosing." When we loose in the spiritual realm, we're unlocking the chains of evil powers and setting people free from their harm and tricks.

Why Do We Need to Bind and Loose?

Well, sometimes there are invisible bad guys in our lives, just like in a superhero story. These bad guys want to make us sad, scared, or do bad things. They try to trick us, just like a villain in a movie. But don't worry; we have the power to stop them!

How to Bind Evil Powers

Imagine you have a special command that makes the bad guys freeze. It's like saying, "Stop right there!" When we use God's power and pray, we can say to the evil powers, "Stop!" We can tell them they can't hurt us or anyone we care about.

Remember, it's not about our own strength but using God's power to stop the bad guys. Just like a superhero using their special powers to save the day!

How to Loose and Set People Free

Now, think of a magical word that can unlock a prisoner's cell and make them free. When we pray and ask God to help us, we can use that magical word to set people free from the bad guys' tricks.

For example, if someone is feeling scared or sad because of the bad guys, we can say, "In Jesus' name, be free!" It's like opening the door to their happiness and peace.

The Secret Weapon: Prayer and Faith

The superpower behind binding and loosing is prayer and faith in God. When we pray, we're talking to God, our superhero. We're telling Him about the bad guys, and He helps us defeat them. It's like calling for backup!

But remember, we need to believe that God is the most powerful superhero ever. When we have faith in Him, our magical rope and key (binding and loosing) work even better!

So, the mystery of binding and loosing demons is like having a superhero power against the bad guys in our lives. We use prayer and faith to tie up the bad guys and set people free. Just like superheroes, we can defeat the evil powers and live in happiness, love, and peace. With God's help, we're unstoppable!

Scripture proclamation

As a Christian, you are the righteousness of God in Christ Jesus. You are called to live a life of faith (**Hebrews 10:38**), and the righteousness of faith speaks (**Romans 10:6**). To walk daily in the provisions of God's Word for your life, you have to maintain a steady stream of faith-filled confessions.

The Bible says that ***death and life are in the power of the tongue...*** (**Proverbs 18:21**). Remaining alive and well depends on what you say. **2 Corinthians 4:13** says, ***"We having*** *the same spirit of faith…also believe, and therefore speak."* Faith's Proclamations are daily attestations to all the wonderful realities of your life in Christ through His Word.

The whole Gospel of Jesus Christ is the gospel of the Word. You proclaim and confess your alliance to the spirit of Christ, then you are redeemed. You are redeemed by acknowledging that we are sinners and that we are in need of a savior. All these things happen when you speak. It is written that you believe, therefore, you speak.

We have adopted the spirit of God through Jesus Christ. God has adopted us into His kingdom through His son Yeshua. The sacrificial lamb is Christ who took our sins to the cross. At the cross is where we lay our infirmities and weaknesses. Every drop of the blood that was spilled on the ground spoke better things for humanity, the people of then, and now, and for the people to come.

We have the blood that speaks better than the blood of Abel. When we proclaim and confess scriptures and the promises of God over our lives, we should do so boldly as people who are redeemed. Even when you are trusting God for your healing, you should enter into his presence with praise and thanksgiving knowing that He did it on the cross. This is an act of faith. Faith is the game changer of all things that seem impossible to change. Through faith, you know that you shall not die but live to declare the goodness of the Lord.

Saints of old had good reports through faith. Jesus Christ stressed faith in His ministry more than anything. Faith is above all. Through it folks, we shall have a good report before the Living God.

Hebrews 11:1-2

1 Now faith is the substance of things hoped for, the evidence of things not seen. 2 For by it the elders obtained a good report.

Hebrews 11:6 But without faith it is impossible to please him: for he that cometh to God

must believe that he is, and that he is a rewarder of them that diligently seek him.

Faith is the believing heart unto the promises of God and His Word. And is exercised through vocalization. The power of life and death is in the tongue. Your mouth is your treasure source. You can choose to speak life, or you can speak death. We are justified by the Word we speak.

Proverb 18:20-21

20 A man's belly shall be satisfied with the fruit of his mouth; and with the

increase of his lips shall he be filled.

21 Death and life are in the power of the tongue: and they that love it shall

eat the fruit thereof.

I usually go out in a public space in my neighborhood to proclaim scripture, decree, and declare the very own Word of God to shift the cycle of evil that has been moving over our community. This is where you a doing warfare prayers against principalities and powers that influence the course of life in your city. You will see breakthroughs and many evil strongholds of evil will be broken.

Many people are caged and blocked from moving forward in life. Marine powers have caged the destinies of many believers. Territorial spirits hovering over the community are introducing all kinds of evil. There are spiritual wickedness in high places.

Ephesians 6:12

12 For we wrestle not against flesh and blood, but against principalities,

against powers, against the rulers of the darkness of this world, against spiritual

wickedness in high places.

I have so much to say about principalities and powers as I have encountered these powers in my town. Many pastors will tell you to look at the pattern of the individual residing in a certain community to map out which strongmen and powers are influencing. While this might true, the holy spirit of God is the revealer of all truth, not some truth, but all truth. For He is the spirit of truth, the spirit of wisdom, and all understanding.

This is called strategic warfare. When you are contending with powers from the sky, you do not deal with them as you would like ordinary demons. Those are principal demons—prince and princess in the spirit. that is why the Devil is called the prince of the power of the air.

Prayer, fasting, and worship will change the atmosphere of many nations. The heavens must invade the territory occupied by the powers of darkness. When the high heavens are in control, everything falls into place; there is breakthrough, miracles, signs, and wonders on earth. The high heavens I am talking about is the third heaven—the dwelling place of the glory of God, the habitation of the redeemed in the Lord.

There is real damage that happens in spirit when praise is your potent weapon of warfare. Paul and Silas serve as an example of the power of praise. Jehoshaphat also.

Apostle Paul and Silas account

In the heart of spiritual warfare, the extraordinary account of Apostle Paul and Silas worshipping in the midnight hour stands as a beacon of inspiration. This story illustrates the unparalleled power of praise when confronted with the darkest forces.

Amidst their unjust imprisonment in Philippi, Paul and Silas defied despair by lifting their voices in praise. Their praise was not a response to favorable circumstances; it was an assertion of unwavering faith in the face of adversity. This teaches us a vital lesson: in the battleground of spiritual warfare, praise is our mighty weapon.

1. **Defying Darkness**: Just as Paul and Silas faced physical chains and imprisonment, we too confront spiritual chains and battles. But as they praised, supernatural forces were unleashed. Their praise shook the prison, broke their chains, and ultimately led to their freedom. In spiritual warfare, praise has the power to break the chains of bondage and release us from spiritual oppression.

2. **Miraculous Victory**: Their midnight praise led to an earthquake, a divine intervention that not only secured their freedom but also transformed their oppressors. The jailer and his household were converted, and the enemy was defeated. Praise, in spiritual warfare, paves the way for miraculous

victories, confounding the schemes of the adversary.

3. **Joyful Resilience**: Paul and Silas found joy amidst suffering, and their praise sustained them through the darkest hours. In spiritual warfare, praise becomes a source of inner peace and unwavering joy, fortifying our spirits in the face of trials.

4. **Witness to the Enemy**: The conversion of the jailer is a testament to the impact of praise as a powerful testimony to the enemy. When we praise in the midst of spiritual battle, it confounds the forces of darkness and draws souls into the light.

In the battleground of spiritual warfare, praise is our mighty weapon. It defies darkness, brings about miraculous victories, fosters joy amidst trials, and serves as a powerful witness to the enemy. Just as Paul and Silas discovered, when we lift our voices in praise, we unleash divine victory in the spiritual realms, ensuring that the forces of light prevail over the forces of darkness.

Here is another inspiring account of the power of praise and proclamation in times of warfare.

Jehoshaphat's account of victory through praise

Jehoshaphat, a revered king of Judah in biblical history, provides us with another remarkable example of overcoming adversity through the power of praise and fasting. His story, found in 2 Chronicles 20, serves as a testament to the effectiveness of these spiritual disciplines in the face of daunting challenges.

Jehoshaphat faced a formidable alliance of enemy nations marching against Judah. Faced with overwhelming odds, he turned to God in prayer, fasting, and praise. This pivotal moment reveals profound lessons for believers today:

1. **Recognition of Helplessness**: Jehoshaphat's first step was to acknowledge his own helplessness. In times of spiritual warfare, recognizing our limitations is crucial. Through fasting, he humbled himself before God, recognizing that victory would come through divine intervention, not human effort alone.

2. **Seeking God's Guidance**: Jehoshaphat's fast was a powerful expression of his earnest seeking of God's guidance. In times of crisis, fasting becomes a powerful channel for seeking divine wisdom and discernment, enabling believers to make sound decisions.

3. **Praise as a Weapon**: As Jehoshaphat's army approached the battlefield, he positioned singers and worshippers at the front lines. Their praise was not only an act of faith but also a spiritual weapon. The enemy forces were thrown into confusion, and they turned on each other. Praise, in this instance, became a catalyst for divine intervention.

4. **Miraculous Victory**: Through fasting, prayer, and praise, God delivered Jehoshaphat and Judah from certain destruction. The enemies were defeated without Judah lifting a sword. This miraculous victory underscores the profound impact of spiritual disciplines in spiritual warfare.

Jehoshaphat's journey reminds us that in times of adversity and spiritual warfare, we can find strength, guidance, and victory through fasting, prayer, and praise. When we recognize our helplessness, seek God's guidance, and wield praise as a weapon, we position ourselves for divine intervention and triumphant outcomes. Jehoshaphat's legacy serves as an enduring testimony to the power of faith, praise, and fasting in the lives of believers, offering hope and inspiration for all facing spiritual battles today.

Proclamation prayer

- I declare today that I am in Christ and Christ is in me!
- Because I am in Christ, I am a new creation; old things have passed away; behold, all things have become new! (2 Corinthians 5:17)
- There is therefore now no condemnation to those who are in Christ Jesus. (Romans 8:1)
- Because Christ is in me, I have victory over the enemy; for greater is He that is in me than he that is in the world. (1 John 4:4)
- I choose to believe God today and walk by faith in His word!
- For whatever is born of God overcomes the world, and this is the victory that has overcome the world, my faith. (1 John 5:4)
- In walking by faith, I please God. (Hebrews 11:6)
- I receive the promises of God into my life today, and it's by these promises I experience the reality of the life God has for me. (2 Peter 1:4)
- I will not be afraid, for it is my Father's good pleasure to give me the kingdom. (Luke 12:32)
- I have not been given the spirit of fear, but of power, and of love, and of a sound mind. (2 Timothy 1:7)
- He has given me richly all things to enjoy. (1 Timothy 6:17)
- I have received all things that pertain to life and godliness. (2 Peter 1:3)
- I have the advantage wherever I go and in whatever I do, because I am seated in heavenly places with Christ. (Ephesians 2:6)

- God has set before me an open door, and whatever door God opens, no man can shut it. (Revelations 3:8)

- I am surrounded by the shield of God's favor. (Psalm 5:12)

- I have favor and good understanding in the sight of God and man. (Proverbs 3:4)

- I am blessed with every spiritual blessing in the heavenly places in Christ Jesus. (Ephesians 1:3)

- Christ became a curse for me, so I am blessed with the blessing of Abraham through Jesus Christ. (Galatians 3:13, 14)

- I am loved by God, and His perfect love casts out fear. (1 John 4:18)

- His love covers a multitude of sins. (1 Peter 4:8)

- Because I am loved by God, I choose to love others.

- I choose to be quick to listen and slow to speak, and slow to wrath. (James 1:19)

- I choose to forgive and to let it go.

- I choose to prefer others before me. I am a peacemaker.

- No weapon formed against me shall prosper, and every tongue that rises against me in judgment, I shall condemn. (Isaiah 54:17)

- No evil shall befall me, and no plague shall come near my dwelling. (Psalm 91:10)

- I am established in righteousness, and am far from oppression and terror, for it shall not come near me. (Isaiah 54:14)

- Sin does not reign over me, for I am not under the law, but under grace. (Romans 6:14)

- I lay aside every weight and the sin that so easily besets me, and I choose to run with endurance, the race that is set before me with my eyes on Jesus, the Author and the finisher of my faith. (Hebrews 12:1, 2)

- I receive an abundance of grace and the gift of righteousness; therefore I reign in life through Jesus Christ. (Romans 5:17)

- I choose what Jesus came to give me -—life and that more abundantly!!! (John 10:10)

- I open my ears to hear what the Spirit of God is saying to me and live under His influence in my life. He will guide me into all truth. (John 16:13)

- The same Spirit that raised my Lord Jesus from the dead lives in me. (Romans 8:11)

- I have the anointing abiding in me and teaching me all things. (1 John 2:27)

- Because I am anointed, I will preach the gospel where I go in word and in deed.

- Signs and wonders follow me because I am a believer.

- I expect the supernatural! I expect God to use me!

- I have length of days, long life, and peace, through the word of God. (Proverbs 3:1, 2)

- The word of God has all the answers for my life.

- I have health because He sent His word and healed me and delivered me from all my destruction. (Psalm 107:20)

- I will bless the Lord and remember all His benefits. He has forgiven all my sins. He has healed all my diseases. He has redeemed my life from destruction. (Psalm 103:3, 4)

- By His stripes I am healed! (Isaiah 53:5)

• Jesus said I have what I desire when I pray because I believe that I receive it! So I believe that I receive. (Mark 11:24)

• He took the limits off, so I put no limits on!

• I let this mind be in me which was also in Christ Jesus. (Philippians 2:5)

• I have the mind of Christ. (1 Corinthians 2:16)

• I commit every thought, word and action to bring glory and honor to the name of Jesus!

• As for me and my house, we will serve the Lord! (Joshua 24:15)

• All my children shall be taught by the Lord and great shall be their peace! (Isaiah 54:13)

• He shall give His angels charge over me and my family to guard, preserve and keep us in all our ways. (Psalm 91:11)

• The blood of Jesus cleanses us and covers our lives!

• Jesus is Lord of my life and all my house!!!

Power in the blood of Jesus

Here are the five testimonies to the blood of Jesus:

• Through the blood of Jesus, I am redeemed out of the hand of the devil.

• Through the blood of Jesus, all my sins are forgiven.

• The blood of Jesus Christ, God's Son, is cleansing me, now and continually, from all sin.

• Through the blood of Jesus, I am justified, made righteous, just-as-if-I'd never sinned.

• Through the blood of Jesus, I am sanctified, made holy, set apart to God.

A warrior in the Lord should be familiar with the mystery of the power of the blood of Jesus. Old saints of the gospel of Jesus Christ were delivered even by mere singing blood songs. Today, this generation has forgotten all that. There is a power in the blood of Jesus!

Personally, I have seen the mighty hand of the Living God when the blood of Christ is evoked or applied. I will be singing songs that talk about the blood of Jesus in the middle of the night, no witch or wizard will dare come to the tent of my house!

You also have to know that the foundation of the kingdom of darkness is laid upon blood sacrifices. Like if you want to conjure up spirits, you have to kill a chicken, dog, or goat. It is all about sacrifices if you also want to be elevated. The agents of Satan, the more they destroy people's lives and the more they kill, the more they will be rewarded by the Devil.

So, the analogy is this, when they are busy drinking human blood to empower themselves to wreak havoc like the women in Revelation filled with the blood of saints, let us allow the blood of the lamb to cleanse us, empower us, set us apart and redeem us from the grip of all evil. You can also cover your city with the blood of Jesus. The blood in the realm of spirit is the light of Jesus Christ—the glory of God. And the blood travels at the highest speed.

The moments you call on the blood; it is done in the realm of spirit. life is spiritual, everything that happens takes place in spirit before manifestation.

We know that the blood of Jesus speaker's better things. The blood speaks better over your life, marriage, finances, career, and many more. The plan of God is to empower and sustain every individual with His glory. A life of lack and poverty is not what God intended. We are redeemed by the precious blood of the Lamb, not only in our sins but in all aspects of our lives we are redeemed, we are healed, we are set apart, we are made righteous and we are more and more for we are the bearer of the light of God—the testimony of Jesus Christ the son of the Living God.

What's more, we are no longer slaves but friends of God. Hallelujah to He Who Loved us and glorified us!

Saving Blood of Jesus songs

1 What can wash away my sin?
Nothing but the blood of Jesus.
What can make me whole again?
Nothing but the blood of Jesus.
Refrain:
O precious is the flow

that makes me white as snow;
no other fount I know;
nothing but the blood of Jesus.
2 For my pardon this I see:
nothing but the blood of Jesus.
For my cleansing this my plea:
nothing but the blood of Jesus. [Refrain]
3 Nothing can for sin atone:
nothing but the blood of Jesus.
Naught of good that I have done:
nothing but the blood of Jesus. [Refrain]
4 This is all my hope and peace:
nothing but the blood of Jesus.
This is all my righteousness:
nothing but the blood of Jesus. [Refrain]
United Methodist Hymnal, 1989

Oh, The Blood Of Jesus Lyrics by Brooklyn Tabernacle

Oh, the blood of Jesus!
Oh, the blood of Jesus!
Oh, the blood of Jesus!
It washes white as snow.
What can wash away my sins?
Nothing but the blood of Jesus.
What can make me whole again?
Nothing but the blood of Jesus.
Oh, the blood of Jesus!
Oh, the blood of Jesus!
Oh, the blood of Jesus!
It washes white as snow.
What can wash away my sins?

Nothing but the blood of Jesus.
What can make me whole again?
Nothing but the blood of Jesus
Jesus' Blood Never Failed Me Yet Lyrics by Jars Of Clay
Jesus' blood never failed me yet
Never failed me yet
Jesus' blood never failed me yet
This one thing I know that He loves me so
Jesus' blood never failed me yet
Never failed me yet
Jesus' blood never failed me yet
This one thing I know that He loves me so
Jesus' blood never failed me yet
Never failed me yet
Jesus' blood never failed me yet
This one thing I know that He loves me so
Jesus' blood won't fail me yet
Won't fail me yet
Won't fail me yet
Jesus' blood never failed me yet
Never failed me yet
Jesus' blood never failed me yet
This one thing I know that He loves me so
Jesus' blood never failed me yet
Never failed me yet
Jesus' blood never failed me yet
This one thing I know that He loves me so
Jesus' blood never failed me yet
Never failed me yet
Jesus' blood never failed me yet

This one thing I know that He loves me so
Jesus' blood
(Won't fail me yet)
Blood
(Won't fail me yet)
His blood
(Won't fail me yet)
Jesus' blood
(Won't fail me yet)
His blood
(Won't fail me yet)
Won't fail me yet
(Won't fail me yet)
Jesus' blood
(Won't fail me yet)
His blood
(Won't fail me yet)
His blood won't fail me
(Won't fail me yet)
This one thing I know
That He loves me so

30 Blood of Jesus Scriptures.

My debt is paid, once and for all

"So Christ was offered once to bear the sins of many. To those who eagerly wait for Him He will appear a second time, apart from sin, for salvation." (Hebrews 9:28)

I am justified

"Much more then, having now been justified by His blood, we shall be saved from wrath through Him. " (Romans 5:9)

I am forgiven

"In Him we have redemption through His blood, the forgiveness of sins, according to the riches of His grace" (Ephesians 1:7)

I am spared from God's wrath

"Much more then, having now been justified by His blood, we shall be saved from wrath through Him. " (Romans 5:9)

I am being spiritually healed; one day even my flesh will be replaced with an incorruptible body

"...who Himself bore our sins in His own body on the tree, that we, having died to sin, might live for righteousness—by whose stripes you were healed." (I Peter 2:24)

I am spiritually alive

"Then Jesus said to them, "Most assuredly, I say to you, unless you eat the flesh of the Son of Man and drink His blood, you have no life in you." (John 6:53)

My judgment has been satisfied and I am at peace with God

"But He was wounded for our transgressions, He was bruised for our iniquities; the chastisement for our peace was upon Him, and by His stripes we are healed." (Isaiah 53:5)

The bloodstream of His people Israel will be purged

"For I will cleanse their blood that I have not cleansed: for the Lord dwells in Zion" (Joel 3:21)

I am cleansed

"But if we walk in the light as He is in the light, we have fellowship with one another, and the blood of Jesus Christ His Son cleanses us from all sin." (I John 1:7)

I have the power to overcome the enemy

"And they overcame him by the blood of the Lamb, and by the word of their testimony, and they loved not their lives unto the death." (Revelation 12:11)

I am no longer under the curse of the law

"Christ has redeemed us from the curse of the law, having become a curse for us (for it is written, "Cursed is everyone who hangs on a tree")." (Galatians 3:13)

I have been reclaimed from the enemy

"In Him we have redemption through His blood, the forgiveness of sins, according to the riches of His grace." (Ephesians 1:7)

I am no longer a stranger to the covenant of promise

"...that at that time you were without Christ, being aliens from the commonwealth of Israel and strangers from the covenants of promise, having no hope and without God in the world. But now in Christ Jesus you who once were far off have been brought near by the blood of Christ." (Ephesians 2:12-13)

The final act of public expiation has been made on my behalf

"For the life of a creature is in the blood, and I have given it to you to make atonement for yourselves on the altar; it is the blood that makes atonement for one's life." (Leviticus 17:11)

I have been moved from the enemy's kingdom into the kingdom of God

"Having disarmed principalities and powers, He made a public spectacle of them, triumphing over them in it." (Colossians 2:15)

. . . .

I HAVE GAINED THE UNMERITED favor of God

"In Him we have redemption through His blood, the forgiveness of sins, according to the riches of His grace." (Ephesians 1:7)

I have been declared righteous

"For He made Him who knew no sin *to be* sin for us, that we might become the righteousness of God in Him." (2 Corinthians 5:21)

I have been justified (just as though I had never sinned)

"being justified freely by His grace through the redemption that is in Christ Jesus,whom God set forth *as* a propitiation by His blood, through faith, to demonstrate His righteousness, because in His forbearance God had passed over the sins that were previously committed..." (Romans 3:24-25)

I am able to come close to God

"But now in Christ Jesus you who once were far off have been brought near by the blood of Christ." (Ephesians 2:13)

I can participate in the sweet communion of remembrance of His sacrifice

"Likewise He also *took* the cup after supper, saying, "This cup *is* the new covenant in My blood, which is shed for you." (Luke 22:20)

My redemption will never perish

"Knowing that you were not redeemed with corruptible things, *like* silver or gold, from your aimless conduct *received* by tradition from your fathers, but with the precious blood of Christ, as of a lamb without blemish and without spot." (1 Peter 1:18-19)

Jesus testifies on my behalf that I am clean

"...and from Jesus Christ, the faithful witness, the firstborn from the dead, and the ruler over the kings of the earth. To Him who loved us and washed us from our sins in His own blood and has made us kings[and priests to His God and Father, to Him *be* glory and dominion forever and ever. Amen." (Revelation 1:5)

I am free

"Stand fast therefore in the liberty by which Christ has made us free, and do not be entangled again with a yoke of bondage." (Galatians 5:1)

I am protected from judgment

"that you shall say, 'It *is* the Passover sacrifice of the Lord, who passed over the houses of the children of Israel in Egypt when He struck the Egyptians and delivered our households.'" So the people bowed their heads and worshiped." (Exodus 12:27)

I am freed from a conscience defiled by guilt

"let us draw near with a true heart in full assurance of faith, having our hearts sprinkled from an evil conscience and our bodies washed with pure water." (Hebrews 10:22)

• • • •

I AM NO LONGER CONDEMNED

"*There is* therefore now no condemnation to those who are in Christ Jesus, who do not walk according to the flesh, but according to the Spirit." (Romans 8:1)

I have been separated from the world and declared holy (wholly) to God

"I have been crucified with Christ; it is no longer I who live, but Christ lives in me; and the *life* which I now live in the flesh I live by faith in the Son of God, who loved me and gave Himself for me." (Galatians 2:20)

I can proclaim total victory

"And they overcame him by the blood of the Lamb, and by the word of their testimony, and they loved not their lives unto the death." (Revelation 12:11)

I can enter boldly into the holiest of holies...and live

"Therefore, brethren, having boldness to enter the Holiest by the blood of Jesus, by a new and living way which He consecrated for us, through the veil, that is, His flesh, and *having* a High Priest over the house of God, let us draw near with a true heart in full assurance of faith, having our hearts sprinkled from an evil conscience and our bodies washed with pure water." (Hebrews 10:19-22)

Psalm 91 prayer declaration over your life.

Personalized.

Psalm 91 Those who live in the shelter of the Most High will find rest in the shadow of the Almighty. This **I** declare about the LORD: He alone is **my** refuge, **my** place of safety; he is **my** God, and **I** trust him. For he will rescue **me** from every trap and protect **me** from deadly disease. He will cover **me** with his feathers. He will shelter **me** with his wings. His faithful promises are **my** armor and protection. **I** will not be afraid of the terrors of the night, nor the arrow that flies in the day. **I** will not dread the disease that stalks in darkness, nor the disaster that strikes at midday. Though a thousand fall at my side, though ten thousand are dying around **me**, these evils will not touch **me**. Just open **my** eyes, and **I** will see how the wicked are punished. If **I** make the LORD **my** refuge, if **I** make the Most High **my** shelter, no evil will conquer **me**; no plague will come near **my** home. For he will order his angels to protect **me** wherever **I** go. They will hold **me** up with their hands so **I** won't even hurt **my** foot on a stone. I will trample upon lions and cobras; **I** will crush fierce lions and serpents under **my** feet! The LORD says, "I will rescue those who love me. I will protect those who trust in my name. When they call on me, I will answer; I will be with **them** in trouble. I will rescue and honor them. I will reward them with a long life and give **them** my salvation."

References

Https://thinke.org/blog/power-of-fasting-and-prayer[1]

War in Heaven by Derek Prince.

Victory in Spiritual Warfare by Thabang Tefo.

https://www.sharefaith.com/blog/2014/07/30-blood-of-jesus/

---

1. https://thinke.org/blog/power-of-fasting-and-prayer

Don't miss out!

Visit the website below and you can sign up to receive emails whenever Johannes Tefo publishes a new book. There's no charge and no obligation.

https://books2read.com/r/B-A-UEZX-BDNXC

BOOKS 2 READ

Connecting independent readers to independent writers.

Did you love *Territorial Spirits: Overcome Evil Strongholds in Your Life And Take Over Your Community With Strategic Warfare And Winning Prayers*? Then you should read *Michael For Warfare*[2] by Johannes Tefo!

In the midst of a world plagued by darkness and evil, a powerful ally stands ready to guide and protect us through the turbulent times ahead. "Michael For Warfare" is a compelling and illuminating exploration of how we can partner with the mighty Archangel Michael in the ultimate battle against malevolent forces, heralding the End Time Move of God.

---

2. https://books2read.com/u/ml6GRZ

3. https://books2read.com/u/ml6GRZ

This captivating book delves into the age-old concept of divine warriors and their pivotal role in the cosmic struggle between good and evil. Author Johannes Tefo offers a unique perspective on Archangel Michael, one of the most renowned celestial warriors, and how we can tap into his divine energy to stand against the rising tide of darkness.

Within these pages, you will embark on a spiritual journey that unveils the secrets of invoking Archangel Michael's protection and guidance. Drawing from ancient texts, mystical traditions, and modern insights, you'll learn how to forge a powerful connection with this benevolent warrior-angel, strengthening your resolve and courage as you face the challenges of our troubled world.

"Michael For Warfare" is a beacon of hope, offering practical advice, heartfelt anecdotes, and inspiring stories that demonstrate the transformative power of aligning with Archangel Michael. As you read this remarkable book, you will discover the tools and knowledge you need to help usher in the End Time Move of God, joining the forces of light to defeat the darkness that threatens our world.

Prepare yourself for a spiritual awakening and be part of a divine alliance that will bring about profound change in the face of adversity. Embrace the wisdom and might of Archangel Michael, and step boldly into the epic battle against evil forces.

Also by Johannes Tefo

Family spiritual Warfare Books
Youth's Guide To Spiritual Warfare
A Women's Guide To Spiritual Warfare

Standalone
Deliver Your Soul From Evil: Self Deliverance Guide
Deliverance From Mind Control: Be Free And Delivered
From Every Marine Demons Of Mind Control
Overcoming Spirit Of Stagnation
The 24: Prophetic Word For This Season 2024 And Beyond
Michael For Warfare
Territorial Spirits: Overcome Evil Strongholds in Your Life
And Take Over Your Community With Strategic Warfare
And Winning Prayers

About the Author

Before he started writing Christian books, Johannes got a graduate degree in Film and Television from university of Johannesburg. After that, just to shake things up, he went to equip himself with religious studies, particularly Christianity, just to have knack about the world beyond the curtains of time. And how this body of Christ has transformed millions of people around the world, not neglecting how sadly the movement has been persecuted from time to time. He now writes full time.